Why Me God?

Because I Ordained Your Steps

Brother Kel Mitchell

Let my story be a blessing
to you and others you love.

Kevin L. Gentry, Dr.

My God Story

9-8-19

Why Me God?

Because I Ordained Your Steps

Kevin L. Hunt, Sr.

Copyright

Books may be purchased by contacting the publisher.

Butterfly Typeface Publishing
PO Box 56193
Little Rock AR 72215
www.butterflytypeface.com

Cover Design: Ministering Moments
Publisher: Butterfly Typeface Publishing
Editor: Ingrid Zacharias
ISBN: 978-1-947656-02-4
ISBN10: 1947656023

1. Religion 2. Self-Help 3. Life Style 4. Spirituality

First Edition
Printed in the United States

Dedication

To my great-grandmother,
Eva Mae Good,
my grandmother Hattie Scott,
and my mother, Eloise Ford Goss.

"Lead by Example"

TABLE OF CONTENTS

Foreword

"A Witness "

One of the most poignant positions in which a person can serve is that of a witness. A witness is one that can attest to the facts that are being presented. I am humbled to have been asked to write the foreword on behalf of my friend, Kevin L. Hunt, Sr. in his first book, Why Me God? I can attest to the fantastic and awesome story contained within the pages of this book. It is a biography of a man that I consider to be a brother.

Kevin and his family are truly brethren in Christ to my family and me. Over the years, he and I have fellowshipped heartily in our *real talk* language, all while confirming the goodness of

God in our lives and speaking the truths of His Encouraging Word throughout our many struggles and shared challenges. In life, we are blessed when God provides us opportunities to build purposeful relationships with our fellow man to work together on the "Team to do God's Will."

No small part of God's special team is Kevin Hunt. I met Kevin during the 2006 Arkansas election cycle. After several years of working in Little Rock's urban market in business sales and marketing positions, I fell upon a unique opportunity to become involved in a gubernatorial campaign. I accepted a role as 2nd District Director of Outreach with the Arkansas Democratic Party. Democratic candidate, Attorney General Mike Beebe was the top of the ticket.

It was my responsibility to provide outreach strategy and execute plans that would result in votes from the minority communities. I had to build a team of go-getters and those that could relate to the minority voters. We had to provide voter education and to create opportunities for the voters in these communities to get to know Mike Beebe and his policy ideas. We did just that, and Kevin was no small part of that team.

Although he came into the campaign as an unpaid volunteer, Kevin's dedication and enthusiasm to contribute could not be overlooked. It was easy to see that he was eager to connect to something meaningful, rewarding, and simply positive. I didn't know much about him other than the fact he'd recently graduated from Philander Smith College. I initially assumed that he was like many other college students or recent graduates that work campaigns to position themselves for jobs, or to add volunteer experiences to their resume. It didn't take long to realize he was not only genuinely committed, but that he had a lot of experience to offer and that there was much more that was beneath the surface. He was obviously "street", which was exactly the dynamic needed to build the outreach team to effectively reach our target audiences. He fit right in and was committed from day one. In fact, Kevin didn't just fit in; he actually *stood out.*

That has likely been the case throughout his life. I'm certain he has always been an asset to the team, a most valuable player.

The work of the campaign was successful, and our candidates won.

The winning officials immediately began transitioning into their perspective offices, building their staffs, and appointing supporters to key positions. During this time The Divine

Hand of God worked strongly in regard to positioning and opportunities that unfolded. God's Word tells us that He causes us to have favor, both with Him and with man. This favor was at work during this time. Although the clear message was given to all campaign workers, "NO GUARANTEES" of job placement, I was not only offered a position on the Governor's staff but worked in his transition office with his leadership team where decisions and placements were being made every day. I tried to help ensure that my campaign team could be placed; I would recommend them when a fitting opportunity was being considered. I was excited that team members like Shaundell Thomas and Howard Himmelbaum were offered positions on the Governor's staff.

Shortly before it was time for Governor Beebe to be sworn in, the new staff began finalizing paperwork and human resource documents pertaining to our pending state employ. One day as I was working in the tiny transition office, one of the team members that had been offered a position, came in to complete her paperwork. She learned of a setback that prevented her from accepting the position that she was offered. I took it personally because she had held a staff position on my team, and I knew the long hours and hard work she'd put in to earn her opportunity for a fresh start - just like everyone else. I was upset at this turn of events and ended up leaving the office for a moment.

After settling down and returning to the office, I received an unexpected call. It was Kevin Hunt. We'd lost touch after the election, and he happened to call my old campaign number. He was just the right person to hear from at that moment. He shared in my disappointment concerning our friend's situation. He was also aware of the important role she'd played. This was Divine intervention, at an appointed time meant to benefit the author of this book. I excitedly shared with him the opportunity for him to be considered for the position. I was happy that this brother could receive the benefit of his dedication and hard work invested that summer.

He was hired as an assistant on the Governor's Communications staff.

As Governor's staffers, we learned to maneuver through the political and governmental platforms to which we were exposed. We were blessed to experience high-level learning about the inner operations of government, politics, legislative processes, and leadership. We were making key contacts and building solid relationships with those in our state who are eager to see changes in their communities.

We were seeking and sharing resource information and connecting our colleagues with contacts throughout the state. Again, Kevin was no small part of the team. He was one of the bright and diverse group of young people which represented the positive attributes of the new Beebe administration, and specifically a representative of our minority community. It was always important to our group of minority staff members that we sought opportunities to build up and support the underserved and underrepresented constituents of our communities; the hard-working people struggling to survive everyday life.

We began to network with leaders to discuss building opportunities for our communities; we aimed to create economic and community empowerment strategies based on data and platforms available to us. Kevin was very instrumental in the overall development of these connections. He gained a reputation within the governor's staff as respectable and reliable, and genuinely considerate of his colleagues. He was well-liked and known throughout the entire capital building.

These reflections were noted only to provide you the context of my ability to provide testimony to the incredible story that you will read in the pages of this book. I didn't know it then, but that positioning would be a pivotal part of the tremendous growth and development in Kevin's career and life's work. I *did* realize that he was a truly genuine person, gifted, and headed toward great things. I was an early encourager of this servant. From that time, I've been blessed to witness the personal dedication he has had to his family, his community, and actually to the very mission of his life. He is committed to *being a testimony to overcoming adversity.*

Looking back, I can see that the humility and overall genuine, good-natured character that I observed was actually a glimpse of the great anointing upon Kevin's life to really impact the world with his testimony. I would never have known when we met and began to work together, the extent of his colorful background. I was amazed to learn of his young life as a junior high school dropout and of his status as GED recipient.

His story of life in the streets: hustling, slanging and gang-banging, and all the destructive behaviors - is unbelievable. I could never have known of his prior incarceration and being an inmate in the state correction systems. From the time I met him, he was not that guy, not in my sight, nor later to any of our colleagues. As stated, I met Kevin just after he had graduated from college. He was volunteering and seeking to connect to a positive path. I had no idea that the focused determination I witnessed, was his means of pushing forward from his personal dark past.

He was always candid about the various inadequacies that he felt, and he began to disclose certain concerns of his past incidents. I began to understand the stories he'd share of some of the challenges he has faced. I could relate to those inept feelings and the thoughts, short-comings he discussed. However, he continued to push past all those road-blocks from his past. He worked with community organizations and has been an advocate for GED obtainment. He gained the respect of his coworkers and received instruction from mentors and those who would guide him along his journey called GROWTH.

If you've ever met or worked with Kevin Hunt, you know he likes to talk. But if you do know him, you have probably also witnessed the quiet evolution of a powerful witness of God's ability to transform a life. As my brother asks the question, "Why me?" he is humbly wondering how God can use a seemingly unconventional vessel like himself.

He is committed to reaching those who need to hear his message of hope. This book offers hope. Kevin's story inspires me. God literally moved this man from a prison cell to exalted places and positions of influence! If his example of hard work and dedication to positive objectives can inspire one young man or woman, no matter where they may currently be, that they can overcome, and live a life where 1.) God can change them, 2.) blessed them, and 3.) use them to bless others; then the question of "Why Me God", is already answered.

I pray that this very hope will be revealed in the lives of each individual who will receive the powerful message, herein written, in this motivational story. As a witness — to God be the glory.

-Sanci Richardson

Acknowledgments

God put people in my path that have provided resources that I needed to make it where I am in my life today:

To my wife, Maggie: Everything about you mirrors the way Christ intended a woman to be. You are more than just my wife, and friend, we are one in Christ. Your commitment to God encourages me. Thank you for upgrading me in so many areas of my life and for your support as we take the next step in God's will. I know you are my Christ mate. I can feel it in my spirit. Love is an action word, and your action says love every day. I love you with everything God has given me today, tomorrow, and forever. You are the lady of my life, Maggie F. Hunt.

To my son: There's not a son on earth I could compare you to because you are every father's dream. A young man of God that continues to seek his presence. I love you, and I'm very proud of you, of course, I tell you every day, but I cannot stress just how proud I am of you. You always have made me feel like the best father a son could have. You never judge me. No matter where you are in life, you can always call on me. I'm glad you know your worth and yet you live humbly and gracefully, only God. Go be great! I love you KJ.

To my mother: Girl you are my hero, I don't know what I would have done without your prayers from the beginning. I know you don't have favorites, but you made me feel like I was the best child a mother could have. I love you, Mother. You are a strong woman and I admire you for that. You and Sonny have been my biggest cheerleaders. You guys mean a lot to me. I love You Eloise (Ford) and Herbert Goss.

To Billy (my father): You are my guy. I have learned so much about myself from being around you. I would not trade my time with you for anything. I'm blessed to be your son and proud that you are my father. You have so much to offer me that I can share with my son and others. I love you and Uncle Wendell. Keep the Hunt alive.

My family: I love *yall* so much! The support you have given me through this process is priceless. No one was prouder of my transformation than you all. I saw and felt the support in everyone eyes that said we are with you. I'll always remember that! Nothing in this world like family, I have the best sisters, brothers, cousins, uncles, aunties, nieces, and nephews in the world. Thank you.

Tommy and Marilyn Brown: You two helped me so much during my journey. I thank you for allowing me to come to your home as many times a week as I needed to. To use your computer so I could write a paper or whatever else I needed to do for school. I love you and your family. Thank you, Marilyn, for being there to help and encourage me.

Curtis Tate (RIP): Thank you for coming to the house to make sure I stayed encouraged.

April Poe: Thanks for all those dinners you provided for me after my grandmother passed. Thanks for reminding me that, "God will take care of you." I love you for that.

Mother Abrams: It's impossible to count the times I have sought your spiritual and political counsel. Without your guidance, I would be still walking in the wilderness. So many of us are in your debt forever. Thank you!

Lumma Norwood: What can I say? You treated me like I was one of your own from day one. I have always felt like I was a part of your family. There's no way I can pay you back for all of those meals (and I enjoyed so many). You are an amazing friend all year round. Love you for everything!

Mr. Lloyd Huskey, Mrs. Bennie (Yeargin) Wallar, Mrs. Pauline Bowles and Mrs. Pamela Boykins: If you all had not had the love of God in you, I wouldn't be here today. You took time from your day regardless of any possible problems of your own. You always encouraged me and spoke kind words. I love you, and because of you, I will always treat others like you all treated me. Thank you for allowing God to use you to help others and myself. You are that village. Love forever!

To everyone who was a part of my walk during my Philander Smith College days: Thank you! I developed some lifelong friendships with a lot of you all. Those days were some of the best days of my life. I'm convinced that no other school in the world could have shown love like you all displayed towards me. You always want to be somewhere where you can grow, and that's what I experienced there.

Sanci Richardson: It was your obedience to God that elevate me to where I am today. You stayed with me through the process, and you saw God's work first hand in my life. You are a strong woman with a positive attitude about life. Your children are blessed to have a reliable mother like you. I have been equally blessed for having your counsel since you hired me all those years ago. Thank you, and I love you for that. Continue to be a blessing to God's people!

Frank Batemen: You have been so supportive from day one. You are a man of God every day, and that is something that is unfortunately rare in this world. Your daily encouragement helped me through a lot of the tough days in my walk. You know the stories. Thank you for being there for me. Love you for that!

To my East End of Little Rock community: When I think about the support and the love I received from you all, I know it can't be matched. I wish I could name each one of you, but there wouldn't be enough pages in this book to do that! From the streets to the State Capitol, you were there all the way. In all I was doing, there was always someone from the neighborhood with me. I love my community, and there's nowhere in the world I would have wanted to grow up but *The East End*...running up and down 6th street. I love you all for life.

Howard: I know you are gone, but I will never forget what you taught me from the campaign to the governor's office. My grassroots and community activism started with you. Much love, you are missed.

To my partners from the North Side of the river: From day one, I mean day one, *yall* never stopped showing love. You have always been *one-hundred* with me. I have so many memories that I enjoy thinking about today. Real stand up guys. I'll never forget that. Thanks for the support and encouragement that I have received over the years during my transformation.

Much love always,

Kevin L. Hunt Sr.

Preface

I grew up in a household full of believers of God Almighty. The women in my life; my mother, grandmother and great-grandmother, all believed in God. There wasn't a shortage of Bibles in my household, and we heard His name every day.

Now my dad, that was a little different; I never heard him say much about God, but I assumed he believed. I know my father's mother and my uncle Wendell believed in God.

My grandmother and others tried to share God with me. My great-grandmother kept the bible right next to her. She was a faithful reader of *The Word* every day. They prayed for all of us, even before I realized what prayer meant for my life. My grandmother and my great-grandmother covered their family with prayer until their last breath. They were the matriarchs of the family in every sense of the word.

Personally, I didn't know anything about God. I remember them trying to make me go to church every Sunday. I went a few times that I can recall, but once I turned a certain age, I can count the number of times I went to church, and I still won't be able to use all my fingers!

I remember going to church with the parents of some of my friends. I really didn't like going to church when I was younger. Sitting in church for a long time wasn't me. Nor did I enjoy getting up early in the morning. Although I didn't grow up attending church, I did grow up in a house with believers.

As a little kid, I remember the church van from Bethesda Baptist Church (formerly *Thomas Memorial Church*) picking up my great-grandmother and others on Sunday mornings.

Even now when I see church vans, I think about how they used to come to the house and pick up my great grandmother for Church. A lot of time my grandmother was working, but there was always somebody praying for us.

So many other things were going on in my home and community that I couldn't focus on Church. I had a challenging childhood.

My parents had their challenges when I was a kid. My dad stayed on one side of the city, and we stayed in *The East End* of Little Rock. They loved all their kids equally. I remember all the good times we had together. As time went on, things changed, but I didn't notice it at the time. It would be a couple of years before I even realized the changes.

No matter what was going on in their life, I always knew that my parents loved their kids.

There was an epidemic that happened in all black communities in Little Rock, especially ours. It hit our home straight on, and we all felt the effects of it.

Luckily my grandmother and my great-grandmother were strong black women who had a stable household. I stayed with them off and on for most of my life. Those hot meals when I came home from school were the best in the world. I miss them today.

When you take the parents out of the household, and you leave grandparents to raise children, the attitude of those children can begin to change. You can see it in their disposition and grades first.

How could I learn, when the people that were my primary teachers really didn't have my best interest as their priority?

Kevin L. Hunt, Sr.

How could I learn, when my thoughts were preoccupied with the things that were going on in my family?

When you consider these things, it is easy to understand why youth fail in school early on.

I wanted to learn, but I couldn't because of the challenges I was hearing about and noticing within my family and community.

When you remove functioning parts from the household, the kids look for guidance on their own.

The first place they look is to their community. I did what people were doing in my community.

I didn't realize we were poor. Everyone in our community was poor. Some had a little more than others, but it wasn't a lot. They were able to provide a bit more like clothing.

We had food, but some kids had food, better clothes, and even a family car.

Until I noticed we didn't have a lot, I really didn't want a lot. However, once I recognized it, I wanted more.

I'm just so thankful today that Reverend Hezekiah Stewart was providing food and assistance then. The Watershed (the first social hospital) helped a lot of communities. Reverend Stewart was a blessing.

I believe if it had not been for the drugs epidemic and institutional racism, I could have been a doctor or a lawyer or a business owner because I was on the right track early on in elementary.

The drugs came in and seemingly wiped the responsibility from my family's mind. The concern for, "I want to make sure that he or she is doing right," left our family. That did not mean our parents didn't love us. It means the drugs had taken precedence over their obligation to care for us.

The drugs hit all of our communities in the United States, not just *The East End* of Little Rock.

I've asked myself a million times, "Why Me God?"

I wanted to know why I went through the things I went through, why did he keep *me*, when so many others perished. Most importantly, I wondered why I ended up where I am now.

Introduction

Why Me God?

My Grandmother Prayed for Me

God has ordained my steps. He has charged me with helping someone, somewhere, to know that their chance at a better future is not gone.

I want to share my story with you about how over the last 16 years, God directed my path and how He has opened doors no man can close, and he has shut doors no man can open.

Throughout my life, I have been faced with many difficult situations.

Some of those situations entailed an unhealthy obsession for the streets, as well as consequences for actions that were my fault. My life went into a downward spiral.

I faced the reality of so many life-changing negative impacts (gang banging, drug distribution, dropping out of middle school, incarceration), that changed my life forever. Fortunately for me, I was able to turn those negativities into a positive outcome.

My message and the purpose of writing this book is to encourage others and let them know that God is ever so present.

There's no way a man would have willingly opened the doors that have been opened for me if it wasn't for God's hands in my life.

Remember, God is up to something good in your life at all times. Whatever that something looks like, God is in control.

To be honest, the reason the book is entitled *Why Me God?* is because I couldn't understand why I was called to share *my* story with others. I didn't realize what was so crucial about *my* past and present life.

The majority of people I know came up the same way I did. I didn't see the significance in *my* transformation.

God kept telling me to write a book about my life. And I kept asking, "Why?"

I'm not a writer, plus, I don't have the patience for that, I argued.

I also didn't qualify to speak to a group of people when I was still learning how to pronounce every word correctly.

Why use *me* as a vessel?

My past is not something I'm proud of, which was the reason I didn't talk about it. Long story short, I wasn't perfect.

Reading this book will give many people, from all walks of life, who face challenges and obstacles, and opportunity to find HOPE in God.

My God story will direct them to whom they should trust and follow. The audiences will consist of more than just individuals who have been incarcerated or just took the wrong turn, but a family member who is looking for a way out for their loved one's current situation.

I understand now that sharing my story of how God has brought me through, with others who have experienced or are currently experiencing similar situations, will remind them that a change is on the way.

God ordained (designed, ordered) my steps so that I could now witness to you that you must trust God's process, and remember that He is working on your behalf, even when you can't see it.

This is my God story.

Gang Life

Chapter One

The Miseducation of the Streets

Being in a gang was stupid.

The gang justified every wrong thing that I did, from the shootings to all the other street crime.

That's what I learned from being in a gang.

There were things I was involved in that I shouldn't have, but I did them because I had no conscience about it and this was the life I chose.

When I look back on it today, I ask myself, "What the heck was I thinking about?"

The shootings, being shot at, and even being shot, were things I really didn't like. I wasn't in love with that part of it, but it was part of me and my reality.

I'm sure my gang activities inspired others to join.

Was I a leader? No. Was I influential? Yes, of course, I was because people who were in my age group, some even younger than me, were looking at me like, "You're cool. You're doing this. So I'm going to do it too."

The gang banging made it easier to be out there shooting each other, trying to kill each other over colors and neighborhoods just to invoke fear in other gangs. It was all so stupid.

I was just as lost as every other gang member in the city.

The devil had us going.

I regret every minute of it. I still have my gang tattoo on my chest, and I plan on removing it or covering it up. But for right now I want to keep it as part of my testimony because when I'm telling my story about my gang life, I like to pat my chest to say here it is – this is a part of my story.

When I rewrite my story, well I'm rewriting it now, I will eventually remove it because it will no longer be a part of me.

I never liked gang banging. It was wrong, and I knew it was wrong, I regret the things I did, but I love the community I come from.

Again, the wrong I was doing was justified because that is the path I choose to travel down. Being in a gang, you are supposed to do these things. You must be tough. You must commit crime. What person in a gang will question you about why you out here shooting over colors? Being involved in criminal activities is a part of the life. If not, then you're not a *gang banger*. Can you see what it does to you? That is why so many of us are incarcerated, along with our possibilities, while we are young.

Gang banging was a part of everything I was doing in the streets. I thought that was cool and that why I couldn't get ahead because I made bad decision after bad decision.

I think about how I sold drugs to people in the street without regards to their color or situation. The drugs I sold not only harmed that person, but it affected their loved ones too.

I wasn't proud of that. I'm still not proud of it.

That's why I'm writing and telling my story; to try and encourage and inspire other people to awaken them to something that will empower people instead of destroying them.

Kevin L. Hunt, Sr.

I thank God for that.

Gang banging was one of the reasons I kept committing crime. Don't let your past define your future.

I joined the gang in Little Rock right before it became popular. That was around the time when I was committing and getting away with other crime, but eventually, I got caught. You can only get away for so long. Sometimes long can be the first time or it can be after years of illegal activities.

The charge was aggravated robbery and attempted capital murder. Those charges sent me to prison.

I was sent to Tucker prison and then to Vernon where I never stopped gang banging. I only got my act together because I wanted to go home when I was scheduled. After a while, I was assigned to work-release, but then I got into some more trouble. This trouble wasn't related to gang banging.

This trouble was related to the whole black and white thing. This guy said something I didn't like, and I hit him across the head. So, they sent me back to Vernon.

I was fortunate enough even after that for things to go in my favor. A few months later I went up for the parole board and I got a year denial. That meant I had to wait an entire year before I could go before them again. When I got that year denial it hurt, and bothered me, but I expected that.

The crazy thing is that when I went up before the parole board, I didn't even know what an appeal was. This goes back to my lack of education, and not being exposed to simple words.

I had dropped out of middle school. The last full grade that I had completed and knew that I'd really learned something was the sixth/seventh grade. I remember finishing the eighth grade but not the ninth. I could not read or write while I was in prison. I may have attempted to read the sports section.

When I was in prison, I had many friends. There was this one guy who told me to write an appeal. I knew nothing about writing an appeal. Again, I had no idea what appeal was.

I was in the barracks with him for a long time. We were pretty cool. Now when I look back on why he was trying to help me out, he knew I couldn't read, write, nor speak well. I'll never forget this. He said, "Man you want me to write an appeal for you?"

I was surprised. "Yeah," I said. "Would you?"

He wrote the appeal for me. I was granted a second chance to go before the board. I went back in front of the parole board in I made parole.

That was God, but at the time I didn't know that was God.

I couldn't believe I made parole. I was a proud man.

I went home without a plan to rise from my situation. It was easy to continue to be involved in gang activity and other things I shouldn't have been involved. Like many, many people, I hadn't learned my lesson.

So of course, I ended up getting into more trouble.

I think I had been out maybe five or six days. I was in North Little Rock with some of my friends.

We were in the car, and the police got behind us and pulled us over. I got out of the car and took off running.

I was wrong, but again I was blessed and fortunate enough that when I ran they didn't find what I called myself throwing away. I went to jail for fleeing and resisting arrest (which is still on my record today).

I did that, but I thank God they didn't find what I had thrown.

I was locked up for a couple of hours until my guy came and got me. I got out and went back to what I knew how to do. I still had not learned my lesson. So many make this mistake daily.

I got in more trouble. I was in a house, and the police raided the house, thankfully no drugs/guns were found. The next few years I was involved in everything you can name, and a whole bunch of other stupid stuff that could have easily landed me in a place worse than prison – the grave.

Now, I know that I was covered so I can do the work I was called to do. I was covered. I could have easily caught a charge and been sent back to prison. I'm thankful that God had a plan for my life.

Thank God for His will.

A Change

Chapter Two

Misplaced Love and Loyalty

Me and my friends hustled in the street. We carried guns that didn't belong to us. To tell you the truth some people carried guns for no reason.

Why did I carry a gun everywhere I went? It's not like I had people riding around looking specifically for me. Yes, I was still active in the gang, but it wasn't like I had one particular enemy.

We carried guns because carrying a gun is required while in a gang. You need protection from the crimes either you commit or someone in your gang commits.

Sometimes the people in your community may do things that cause you to be a victim by association. Another gang could retaliate on you merely because of your affiliation. Where's the love in that? Look how vulnerable they leave you. Where is the love in that?

Even if you really aren't fully or actively *gangbanging* some people would still *act* like they were in a gang. You had to be 'gang-ish' to fit in. You had to do things like; throw up signs and talk the language.

This was so ridiculous and crazy.

We did a lot of stupid things that didn't require any common sense. Well, it should have, but we didn't apply any.

I did a lot of illegal things that could have easily landed me in jail. Gang life involves all types of crimes such as robberies, shootings, selling drugs, car thefts, breaking into houses, etc. You don't have to be in a gang to commit these crimes, but it justifies your action if you are.

At one point, I was proud to be in a gang. We were always going somewhere representing our neighborhood, pounding on our chest believing that we were untouchable. The reality to that was that we weren't because *homeys* were dying everywhere.

But after all the stuff that had happened in the gang world, it started to bother me. I had begun to come to my senses. I'm not saying I stop hustling or carrying a gun, but I was going to stop doing stupid things like shooting at people just because of the color they were wearing.

The gang activity mindset was always cynical of life, all the time. I couldn't see anything positive about anything because I was in an *I don't care* mode. I thought the gang loved me. But the truth is, you don't get love from a gang, you get love from an individual.

And this is where we were lost.

They always said the gang showed you love, but no it's the individuals that showed you love. You have to remember that within the gang organization fighting, stabbing, robberies, stealing, and murder happens within that group of childhood friends.

We all had our own guys. There were cliques within the gang and cliques within the cliques. There was division and will always be division. We may hurt other groups, but we also hurt each other, just not as much as we did others.

So it wasn't the gang that gave love. The love came from the individual that you trusted. Many times, you already trusted that person before joining that gang. People don't understand this.

Ignorance of the truth caused me and others to do some things for the love of the gang.

Thank God He led me away from a lot of unnecessary stuff.

I stopped carrying guns every day. I stopped seeking to commit criminal activities. I was tired of hiding drugs, throwing guns out of car windows when the cops got behind us. I was tired of being in houses when the narcotics team kicked the door down. I was tired of jumping out of cars and running. I was tired of being on the block and having to take off running at a moment's notice.

Who in their right mind wants to continue to live like that? Who wants to traffic drugs all around the city?

I was maturing, but still had a way to go before I removed that lie out of my system (the lie was that this was the only thing I would ever be able to do with my life).

All those things I did were byproducts of the life I'd led. I didn't believe I could do anything else because I had no education and I was now a felon.

There weren't any doctors, lawyers, nurses or fortune 500 business owners in our community. Our community was permeated with ex-cons, drug users, dropouts, drug dealers, homeless people, very old houses and very low wage workers.

Some of us made it out, but there were more of us that didn't.

So many of us in our community never finished high school. Some never made it to high school, including me.

I was never an evil person. I had a good heart. Most of the people in my community had amazing love for each other. We are good people. We just made plenty of bad decisions.

Our current situation at the time forced us to indulge in crimes.

Do you think I'm proud of the shootings? Shooting at others and being shot at by others is not something to boast. Do you think I'm proud of selling drugs, especially to sick and pregnant women?

I knew it was hurting their family because it was hurting mine.

Do you think I'm proud of the crime I committed? Do you think I'm proud of being shot or listening to bullets flying all over me? Do you think I'm proud about some of my closest friends getting killed, or my partners doing more years in prison than the number of years they lived free?

The answer to these questions is clear, NO!

I'm trying to tell you it's not worth it. If you never experience any of these things, please don't.

You have your life to lose.

Everybody won't make it out once they get in. We will never know who will make it out and who won't.

Only God knows.

Education

Chapter Three

He Covered Me

My grandmother Hattie Scott, passed in 2001. As I look back upon it now, I realize God had been trying to get my attention before that, but nothing up to that point had worked.

I was still doing nothing.

I had a couple of best friends who passed away too. Some had gone to prison. Others got caught up in drugs. So, it seemed like God was trying to get my attention then, but none of that worked.

It wasn't that I didn't love them, but those things didn't break me down like the death of my grandmother did.

It hurt me so bad, but not just because she was dead (which that hurt very badly), but because of all the empty promises I had made to her.

From maybe as early as 1994, I wasn't doing very much of anything. I had a job because at the time it was a requirement of my parole officer. I didn't work because I wanted to, I worked because I was obligated.

I was still doing a lot of other things in the streets that were illegal, but God covered me.

During that time, my grandmother kept urging me to go back to school. She would say, "Kevin baby, won't you just go back to school."

When she'd say that I'd just brush her off and say, "I'm going back one day Granny. I'm going back."

I said that so many times. It wasn't that she asked me that every day, but enough times that it began to seem like it was every day!

She did that from the mid-90s all the way up until her death.

I would tell her I would go back just to say it, but the truth was I had no intention of going back to school because I didn't feel like I could compete in the classroom. I was afraid of school. I knew I was illiterate because I couldn't read, write, or speak well and my thinking was horrible.

I believed that there was nothing I could do with my life other then what I was doing.

The lack of education and low self-esteem coupled with the poverty I saw everywhere I looked, left me without a positive vision for my life.

The only vision I had was of the street game and what it could offer me.

I always felt my day of destruction would be coming soon. It could have been in the form of life imprisonment, paralysis, or even death. I had a feeling that my time was coming.

After seeing so many of my friends' fall victim to the streets, I had to expect mine to follow if I didn't do something.

I had invested everything I had hustling in the streets. Hopeless thinking equated to physical and mental blindness. I couldn't see my mind nor body doing anything else. I didn't have confidence or hope for a future that was bright.

What bothered me the most was not knowing how to read. I don't wish that on anyone. The inability to read can limit you from accomplishing a lot of things in life.

Kevin L. Hunt, Sr.

The failure to read affects your self-esteem and pride.

I remember scrolling through newspapers, magazines, and documents, without an understanding of anything that I saw printed.

It wasn't that I didn't understand some words. I was only able to understand what I had learned the last year I remember focusing in school which was between the 6th and 8th grades.

My conversation about anything was very limited because of my poor use of the English language.

How could I communicate what I just heard or partially read?

We all know someone who can't read, whether it is a family member or friend.

There is hope for them. I know it. Just look at me.

Kevin L. Hunt, Sr.

I remember others informing me of companies that were hiring. In some cases, they would even bring me an application to complete. I was ashamed. My pride wouldn't let me tell them that I couldn't fill out the application. I always told them either I was going to return the completed form or go to the company and apply there. 100% of the time I never filled it out or went to the site, but I always told them I did. I lied over and over.

My confidence and self-esteem were low, but my street IQ was working overtime.

I wasn't afraid of the outcome or the ramifications or using correct grammar because the streets didn't require it. My conversations were about guns, drugs, shootings, women, cars, and things we encountered in our communities.

Not being able to pronounce words was, however, a detriment to my social life.

I remember when one of my friends recognized that I couldn't read. He came over to the house to share the Word of God with me. Somewhere in that visit, I was trying to read God's Word.

Years later he told me that was when he noticed. He said to himself, "Hunt can't read."

I appreciate him for that story. It helps me to see how far I've come.

During that time, you could see the glory of God all over his life. Things were going well for him.

I remember thinking, *I want that peace.*

Back to The Story

Grandmother Hattie knew that going back to school would be the start of a change in my life.

Every time she would ask me about school, I would lie to her because I didn't want to hurt her feelings. I loved her so much that I couldn't tell her the truth, so I gave her false hope. I would have the conversation with her about going back just to please her

"Yes, Grandma I'm going back to school because I've got to do something else," I'd say knowing all along that I had no intention of doing it.

The truth is I was afraid to go back to school. I was enjoying what I was doing. I didn't think I needed to go back to school. I didn't think I could go back to school and obtain a GED.

Grandmother believed in education. She felt like I needed to stop doing the things I was doing. She believed I could get an education and change my life.

My great-grandmother would watch and listen to me telling my grandmother these lies and looking back on it now I wonder did my great-grandmother believe it?

The funny thing is that my great-grandmother died a couple of years after my grandmother. She was around to see me begin the change. My great-grandmother saw me get my GED. She knew about me enrolling in college too. She wasn't around when I earned my Bachelors in 2006 and Master's degrees in 2015, but she had a chance to see me begin the journey.

Both of my grandmothers are in paradise waiting for the second coming of my LORD and savior Jesus Christ.

I believe all those years I lied to my grandmother, telling her I was going to go back when I had no intention of going back became a self-fulfilling prophecy. I'd said that I would.

I didn't go when she was alive, but I went on, and I finished! I was speaking it into existence.

It was her death that pushed me to do what I'd promised her I was going to do. All I could think about was all the times I'd told her I was going back to school. That bothered me. It really bothered me.

In 2001, I knew of God, but I didn't know God Himself. I knew about Christ, but I didn't know Christ Himself. I don't think I had a scripture in my mind that I could have quoted. For one, I couldn't read to the level of the NIV, and honestly, I don't even think I tried to read it.

At that time, I had not been going to anyone's church. I wasn't doing any praying. But I tried to communicate with some of my friends who knew God.

So, when my grandmother died, it was like so much fell on me. I felt really bad. I felt like a liar. I had lied to someone who loved me and had wanted me to do something with my life.

So, my hurt was a mental one because I didn't fulfill a promise. All I could think about was that it was bad enough she was dead, but what hurt more was that I'd lied to her. *Why didn't I just tell her that I wasn't going?* I never told her that. I always told her I was going to go back to school.

She knew what was best for me, just like millions and millions of other grandmothers know. My great-grandmother knew. My mother knew too. But I didn't listen.

I knew God was trying to get my attention when some of my closest friends were killed back to back.

It was very hard going to the funeral of the guys you came up with in the streets. A few of my friends went on to prison. My banging clique of friends was getting small. But still, I didn't make a change.

When my grandmother passed, after all the things I'd gone through, it was *her* death that broke me down.

Her death caused me to think about going back to school. I wanted to fulfill a promise.

I can't recall how long after my Grandmother's death, but I sat in her room watching TV. It was a guy preaching on TV. He was talking about how our testimony was not for ourselves but was for someone else. He was talking about God and that everyone had to die.

That sermon made me think about God a little bit more. From that point on, I found myself wanting to *do something* with my life.

My grandmother's death gave me life, keep reading.

Chapter Four

Fulfilling a Promise

I made up in my mind that I wanted to do something with my life. I wanted to get my GED. I wanted to do it for my grandmother.

I went to my friends and told them, "Hey, let's all go get our GED."

They all agreed, and it made me feel good that I'd mobilized and influenced a group of guys to do something that would benefit us.

This was during the weekend. That following Monday I was excited about the possibility of all of us going at one time. Well when I spoke with everyone who had agreed on Friday, they all bailed out on me that Monday. No one wanted to make that sacrifice.

I went back to my grandmother's house, and the doubts started. A lot of reasons for not doing it began to come to my mind, but the way I felt about my grandmother and about what she'd wanted me to do with my life encouraged me to push past those thoughts. I made up my mind that I was going to go without them.

Thank God!

The next Monday, I drove to Shorter College Adult Education Center in North Little Rock Arkansas, and I sat in my car in the parking lot awhile. I was thinking; *I really don't want to go in there.*

Now I know that was just the devil trying to prevent me from having what was inevitable for my life based on where I am right now. The devil couldn't see the future, but he knew that God had something for me, so he was encouraging me not to go. I sat in the car thinking; *I'm not going in here. This is not for me. I'm not even doing this for myself. I'm doing this for my grandmother.*

I really wasn't encouraged. I don't know how long I sat there in that parking lot, but I know that I was close to leaving that place.

I thank God because the next thing I know, I was reaching out and opening the door, not to my car, but walking inside the college! Even as I stepped inside, I was still trying to convince myself not to go any further.

As I walked in, there was no one in there at the time. I was just walking. I don't know what made me start walking upstairs, but as I was walking up the stairs and neared the top there appeared a guy. "Can I help you young man?" he asked.

I was like, "No, No." But he pushed me even then. I guess I looked confused, but I think he saw something in me.

Mr. Lloyd Huskey, now a good friend of mine, pushed me from the beginning and he has mentored me since 2001. I don't think there was no one better for me at that particular time. We stopped and talked, and he shared a few things with me.

He told me they could help me, gave me some encouraging words, and he walked me into the administration building where I met Mrs. Pamela Boykins.

She and I talked for a minute and then she signed me up for the classes. She always told me, "Kevin, you're doing the right thing."

Thank you for that Mrs. Pamela Boykins. Everything was happening so fast. I needed her encouragement and support.

Mr. Huskey directed me to a classroom where I met Mrs. Pualine Bowles. I love this lady. My God, she was an angel. She loved on me, encouraged me, inspired me. She motivated me. She told me I could do it.

That was the first part of the class.

For the second part, God had another God-fearing woman, Mrs. Bennie (Yeargin) Waller waiting to show me the same love and consideration as Mr. Huskey and Mrs. Pamela Boykins.

Mrs. Waller loved on me. She encouraged and empowered me. She not only showed me I *could* do it, but she also showed me *how* to do it (Proverbs 27:17). She made me believe that I could do it - all within that first hour of me being there! (Philippians 4:19) (2 Corinthians 12:9).

I still had the worse attitude in the world.

It would take them to tell you, but I didn't want to be bothered. I thought I knew everything, but the truth is I was afraid. I knew I couldn't read or write, but I was afraid to confess that. I lived in a world that said I couldn't do it, but they told me "...with God all things are possible." (Matthew 19:26)

Ironically, they were smart enough to know that I was afraid. They knew it off the top! God put something in them for me. They started showing me that I could read. Yes, there were things I needed to tighten up and sharpen up on, and that's what they did for me.

First, they built my confidence by telling me that I could do it and then asking me to let them show me how.

I fought them for a while, but after a few more days, I was still going. I wasn't the best student in the world, but they kept loving on me.

I really hated when they would say, "It's going to be alright baby." For some reason, I hated that in my heart. I hated it. It wasn't like I didn't recognize that it was love. I knew love from my family and community, but I think it was just the devil using that feeling to motivate me to get up and walk away and never come back.

The devil had a feeling that God had something for me and he wanted to keep me from it.

They kept telling me they loved me and that they were going to help me. Mr. Huskey kept coming in and reinforcing what they were telling me. I was encouraged. I felt good.

One day I was in class, and I thought, *Man, what would my grandmother think about this?*

My mother knew I was in class and she was happy and proud. My great-grandmother knew about it, and she was happy and proud too.

Marilyn Brown knew about it. Curtis Tate knew about it. April Poe knew about it. They were all part of my community of close friends and family. They were that motivation in my neighborhood that I needed. They were so happy that I was getting my GED.

Because of their support, I felt empowered. Now I *wanted* my GED. I *wanted* to read, write, spell, and speak. Those people, Mrs. Bowles, Mrs. Waller, and Mr. Huskey, encouraged and showed me the areas where I needed improvement.

But they needed me to remain confident. I needed to keep coming. I needed to show up every day. I had to allow them to do their job. I had to let them love on me. I had to allow God to love on me.

And that's what I did.

I came every day - proudly. I stayed over as long as I needed to. I listened. I raised my hand and asked questions. I did my homework. I did my part.

It wasn't like that when I first got there. I fought them until I realized they were there to help me and not hurt me. It was Mr. Husky who shared that revelation with me.

Other teachers helped me, but Mrs. Bowles, Mrs. Pamela Boykins, Mrs. Waller, and Mr. Huskey are the ones that stood out. They were the ones who loved on me the most.

I felt good, and when I reflect back on that time in my life, I just know that God put them in my life to help.

Months passed, and finally, I was ready to take the pretest to see if I was prepared to take the actual test. I felt like I could read and write. Was

I the best? No, but I was a long way from where I started. A lot of that was because now I had confidence in my ability because of the confidence-building team God put in my path. (Proverbs 3: 6)

Before, I didn't believe I could do it. I was afraid, but they showed and challenged me to this new level of confidence. They reminded me that if I kept reading and keep practicing that I could go on to the next level.

So, I took and passed the pretest in 2001. In winter of 2001, I passed my GED test. That was the best thing that could have ever happen to me at that time.

I cried, not in front of them, but I cried.

I pulled out my diploma and looked at it. I was so happy! I was so proud!

I came in afraid. I came in defeated. I came in with low self-esteem. I came in knowing I *couldn't* do this. I came in doing it for someone else. I came in knowing I would quit. But I stayed. God made me stay.

He surrounded me with His people, people that He had selected before I knew it was God Jeremiah 29:11. He loved on them, so it was easy for them to love on a stranger. It was a challenge on my end, but He prepared me for roadblocks while I was going to school, so that I could stay focused.

And I passed that test.

I remember sitting in the room with Mrs. Waller, Mrs. Bowles, and Mr. Huskey. They were so proud of me. After I passed that test, they started talking to me about going to college.

In my mind, I was like, *College. Did they say college?*

I knew I wasn't college material, but in their minds, they knew that I was. They knew that if I stayed on the path, stayed focused, continued to want to learn how to read, write, and continued to believe in myself, I could compete in a classroom.

So, before I left that room, I told them that I was going to go to college.

They encouraged me to go sign up at Philander Smith College. They told me I would love it there and that I would meet people who have walked the same path that I had walked. I was assured that there were teachers just like them at Philander.

My diploma was the evidence I needed to prove that I could compete in the classroom. There was evidence that hard work paid off. That evidence was me.

So, I went over to Philander Smith College and signed up. When I enrolled, I was afraid. Not only because it was the biggest step in my life, but also because I didn't know what was going to happen. I was afraid of the uncertainty. I had heard about how hard college work was, and I was allowing that fear to cause doubt about what could be.

The question I continued to ask myself was, *are you ready, and if so are you sure?*

Even after obtaining my diploma I continued to attend to Shorter College Adult Education Center because I understood there was so much I still needed to learn. It was months before college would start for me. Being around my Shorter College support system kept me confident.

School started, and yes, I was very nervous, but I went anyway.

The advice they gave me was that I should surround myself with people who were going to school for the right reasons. And that's what I did. There were so many people who were going to school for the right reasons. It was a blessing that I connected with people who were committed and were on a mission.

It didn't matter if they were a junior, senior, freshman, or sophomore; they knew they were going to graduate. It wasn't a matter of 'if' they would graduate college. They knew they would.

I continued to do that.

My first semester, I did well. I started out in intermediate classes. That was no problem for me because I needed those classes to prepare me for what to expect in the other classes and I did well. I went to summer school every summer until I graduated. By the time I was a senior, I didn't have the pressure on me to load up on classes.

I don't want you to think that life didn't have its expected/unexpected challenges. Let me say this; there were many times I wanted to give up. There was always a part of me asking, *what are you doing, why are you here, you know they not going to hire you with your background.*

You have to remember; I had to go back home after my classes. I didn't live on campus. My reality during school hours was different than my reality in the community.

Everything I was trying not to be anymore was what I was around every day. The pressure to continue doing what I was trying to walk away from was at my front door Monday to Monday, no days off.

Kevin L. Hunt, Sr.

My phone number had not changed, my family was here, and my childhood friends remained the same.

How could I stay focused? Crime, violence, and drugs were a part of my conversation every day.

Only God could have been working in my favor because there were challenges before me that I had never experienced in my life. The devil was at work.

There were plenty of challenges while at school too.

In some cases, I was consuming what was going on in my community to the point that it affected my focus while in school.

Not everything was bad. We had some trailblazers to come out of *The East End*.

All my grades weren't A's and B's. I never failed one class. I had to work my butt off just to past those classes!

With all of my effort and dedication, I still allowed small things to distract me from what I was trying to accomplish. But not to the point where I lost focus on why I was there. There were instructors and faculty's members that really wanted the best for each student. Their concerns about my personal life were so important to me at that time.

It didn't take a rocket scientist to see there was things going in my life that I needed to get a handle on. When you have people giving you sound advice, based on their observation of what you *could* become, embrace it!

I listened to their observation, and I made changes in my life so that I could finish what I started.

God will always put people in your life for every purpose He has for you.

It was hard to walk away from the people I had spent my life with and loved. I couldn't do it on my own and God knew it.

Slowly God removed me from people/things that would have caused me to stumble. Some things were in place for me to draw closer to Him.

The friends that remained in my life during the transition supported me from the beginning to the end. The love I received from them pushed me and encouraged me when doubt permeated my thoughts. Those are my guys for life, my brothers.

I can't tell you how much love I have for those guys and girls, old and young.

I remember when Juan and Money were there when I walked across the stage receiving my GED Diploma at Shorter College Adult Education Center. That meant a lot to me for a lot of reasons. They have supported me while I've been on this journey.

They supported me from undergrad, grad school, the governor's office, writing this book, my nonprofit and are still supporting whatever I do.

That's love.

There were others that supported me like my cousin Allen (big time supporter), my (natural) Bolo from day one as well and my north-side Homie, Cap. If I tried to name them all, I'm sure you would stop reading.

From 6 & Bond to Dix, I had support, old and young. They know who they are. Thank for that support. Your boy needed it and appreciated it.

***

I attended Philander from August 2002 to May 2006, earned my credits, and finished with a 3.0 plus GPA!

Oh, my goodness!

You can't tell me that God wasn't with me through that whole time. My reading, writing, speaking, and confidence had increased by 100%.

When you surround yourself with young men and women who can read and write, that encourages you to want to do the same. Was I where I wanted to be? No. But I was surely a long way from where I started.

In some cases, I had some tough times and felt like I wanted to give up, but I didn't.

Some of my professors challenged me. One, in particular, told me that he wouldn't hire me. But that was encouraging criticism. He knew that I could do better.

It's wasn't like I was failing his class. He just knew I had more in me. I needed that talk, seriously.

Was I a biology specialist? No, but I made sure I got all the extra credit, turned in all of my homework, did everything I was supposed to do to make sure I passed the class. This was how I approached every class that was challenging. I worked my butt off. I had never worked so hard. I made the Honor Roll during my time there!

Graduating from Philander Smith College in 2006 with a GPA of 3+ was great, but more importantly; I have confidence in myself academically! I believed!

2006 was one of the greatest moments in my life!

I invited all my friends and family to come to my college graduation. It seemed like my whole community came out to support me. They were so loud. There were so many of my people there. It was amazing.

When I walked across that stage everyone, (my parents, family, and friends, old and young) applauded and celebrated because I had achieved something!

All of them knew where I came from, not *just* the community, but from a place in my life of not knowing how to read, write, or spell to earning a bachelor's degree and becoming a critical thinker! I had hope!

When I left the graduation, I went to the neighborhood projects in *The East End* where I knew everybody would be, got out of the car with my cap and gown on and I yelled, "Yeah!"

There were so many people who came out to support me. People came out of their houses and celebrated with me. It was a glorious time.

We talked and laughed in the hot sun for a while. It was finally hitting me that I had graduated from college (Jeremiah 29:11).

I was on such a high. It caused me to want to inspire and encourage other people to go back to school. I wanted them to know if I could do it, they could too.

Ministry

Chapter Five

The Peace of God

In 2004 I could feel the double-edged sword calling me more and more. People were talking about God to me that I had never mentioned Him before. I found myself listening to TV ministry, but it took me awhile to attend someone's church on my own. I remember trying to go to one church, but I wasn't ready, and I didn't feel right, so I left.

In early spring of 2005, I visited Second Baptist Church in Little Rock. One of my good friends and supporters, Marcus Stephens, was attending there. He had just started going and was bragging about this young preacher, so he invited me. That one-day changed my life, and I never stopped attending.

In 2006 I got baptized. My mother and other family members were there to see me go under as a sinner and come up a new creature. Mother was so excited about the transformation of her son. I thank the Lord for all of her prayers because I don't think I could have done it without her leading by example.

This was the beginning of my spiritual growth. This was the turning point. During this time, I really didn't recognize God's presence in my life as I do now.

Under the leadership of Dr. Kevin A. Kelly – Senior Pastor of Second Baptist Church, I learned a lot about God and who He was. If you wanted to learn about God and what he expects from you, everything you needed is at Second Baptist Church. I can't even begin to tell you how committed I was. The services were powerful. I was hungry, and Pastor Kelly fed us all.

Bible study on Wednesday night was always what I needed it to be and Sunday school with Dr. Carla Morris, Associate Minister at Second Baptist Church was a blessing. The way she shared God's word with us left me convinced that Sunday school should be mandatory.

The love I received from the Second Baptist congregation was without judgment. My infant days as a follower of my LORD Jesus Christ have grown, and now I'm a mature follower of Christ.

One thing I remembered hearing from the few times attending church with my grandmother, was how the devil is *always* busy and looking to devour. He knew God had something in store for me. The enemy didn't know *what*, but he knew it was *big*.

Traps were set-up for me and in some cases I was in places I shouldn't have been, but 90% of the time the Spirit had me on track. I was always covered, and I thank God for that because the enemy is real. However, God had me covered.

I thank God for wisdom, knowledge, and understanding. I thank Him for the council of His people. He covered me. He covered me. That's all I'm going to say because I can't say it enough.

I knew who God was, but I didn't have a personal relationship with Him until I got older. It wasn't until I acknowledged whom God was and got baptized that my relationship with Him changed. It was a struggle at first because I was trying to figure out what I was supposed to do and how I was supposed to act. I was trying to figure out if I really believed in God and if I really believed in what everybody said about Him. I had some questions, but I stayed with it.

God had already been working on me. He'd already been guiding my steps, but I didn't realize it at the time.

By the time I realize that God was working in my life, I'd already earned my GED and I was going into my senior year of college.

I didn't always realize the meaning of God was with me all that time. I didn't fully recognize the presence of God in my life like I feel his presence now. During that time, I was becoming more knowledgeable about God, but I still wasn't where I needed to be in prayer and offering. I wasn't reading every day, but I had a relationship with Christ. I felt the presence of God.

My mother was praying and praising God for what He had done for me. People whom I had met at school (teachers and even maintenance staff) were helping me through the tough times, and they continued to steer me in the direction of God. Over and over again it was, "God Almighty. God Almighty. God Almighty."

As I continued to seek God, I began to have a better understanding of Him.

In 2006 I could see the difference in my life. It was a good feeling, and that feeling drew me closer to God.

I was in college when I got baptized. I started going to church more, and I was really feeling good about my relationship with God. I was getting to know Him more. I was going to every service that I could. God was really on me, loving on me, even though I didn't really acknowledge Him as much as I thought I should have, but He still loved on me.

Over the years the relationship just grew.

As I look back on it now, I can see that He was with me because He covered me through school. There were some challenges at school. There were times when I didn't think I would finish a paper on time or I didn't feel like I studied well enough, but God made a way.

Sometimes when I knew I couldn't or really didn't understand the big things, God gave me the foresight to do all the small things.

For example, I struggled with Biology, but I made sure to turn in all my homework, attend lab, and attend class every day. Those *little* things helped me to be able to pass that class and make a low C which was better than a D! Biology wasn't my thing, but I made sure to do all the things that I could, and they added up. So just in case I didn't do well on the tests, I could still earn a passing grade.

Now when I reflect back on it, that was just all God. He gave me that mindset to try and do the things I could do, instead of giving up. In that way, He was loving on me. He got me through my junior and senior year of college.

Kevin L. Hunt, Sr.

I continued to go to church, but I still hadn't learned the concept of Christianity. I just knew who Christ was and who God was, but I wasn't into 'speak it, seek it' yet because I hadn't got there yet. I was still a baby, drinking milk.

By 2006, I had graduated from college and that's when God really started showing more of his presence in my life. He began to show me the direction He had for my life.

I graduated from college and didn't know what I was going to do. I knew I already had so much against me. After graduation, I was led to the Arkansas Department of Finance to apply for a job.

There I met a very nice, concerned, and loving lady name Ms. Taylor who worked there. I told her that I had just graduated and that I was looking for a job. I also told her that I had been previously incarcerated and that there were things on my record. She was so real with me about the chance of getting hired, but what she did next changed the trajectory of my life.

She said, "I have a friend that works for a guy that's running for the governor's office in Arkansas. Go volunteer for his campaign so you can meet people, gain experience, and if he wins, maybe you can get your record wiped clean."

I took her advice and called her friend, who later became a good friend of mine. When I called her, she said, "Come by the office and fill out some paperwork."

When I arrived, she came down, introduced herself and I filled out the papers and left. A couple of days later I received a call to come volunteer at the North Little Rock office.

God was making moves. He was working behind the scene.

Kevin L. Hunt, Sr.

"Trust in the Lord with all your heart ..." (Proverbs 3:5)

His direction led me to volunteer for the campaign of then-Attorney General Mike Beebe. After volunteering for maybe less than two-weeks, God sent Sanci Richardson to offer me a part-time job, with part-time pay, but full-time hours. I didn't want to take this job because I was there for other reasons, but I remembered something one of my professors had said to me. He said, "I wouldn't hire you. You're not ready. You have to learn how to make sacrifices in life."

So even though this job wasn't what I wanted, I accepted it.

I worked hard for her and earned a friend, a woman of God, a *Big Sis*, and a mentor in Sanci Richardson. God put her in my path. I know that now. I'm so glad she was obedient when He said, "Hire Kevin."

Kevin L. Hunt, Sr.
114

I never asked her what made her hire me. I knew there were other volunteers before me who were qualified, yet she chose me.

Mike Beebe won the office of governor, and I thought that would be the end of that relationship. I knew I couldn't work for him because of my past. However, what happens next is just another testimony of how God directed my path.

I was at a high point in my life. I had learned so much and met people who otherwise would not have spent one second with me. Many relationships were forged during that campaign. Most still exist today.

I went from someone who was from a low-income family, couldn't read or spell, had low self-esteem to working on a gubernatorial campaign. That was nothing but God to take me from all that to where I found myself – with a

GED, a college diploma and an active participant in assisting Mike Beebe in his election for governor.

After the campaign, I started applying for jobs all over the city. I got a call back very quickly from a company that people said would have been a good fit for me fresh out of college. They scheduled a phone interview shortly afterward, and it went very well. I received a second interview with one of the supervisors, and we went over the opportunities they offered.

During that conversation, the supervisor informed me that the position I applied for was in Texas. I would have to move to Texas.

I asked him, "Is there anything in Little Rock?"

"No," he said. "Take a couple of days to think about it and let me know your decision."

I didn't need a couple of days because I had a young son that I was not going to leave. That was the end of that interview. I wanted to be around my son.

Immediately after getting off the phone with him I called Sanci hoping she would have some leads on some jobs.

Another God moment.

When I called her, she said, "Kevin we got one position in the governor's office that was offered to two other people."

She told me to hold on while she gave the phone to someone else. He got on the phone, introduced himself and then said, "Can you come in and fill out an application?"

I said yes, and he gave the phone back to Sanci.

"Sanci, you know I can't work for the governor's office," I said. "Does the application have *the box*?"

The box is in reference to the question that asks if you have a felony on your record.

She said she didn't remember because it had been a while since she had filled out her application.

I was nervous. I was basically trying to talk myself out of the embarrassment. Thank God He wouldn't allow me to run from the plan He had for me.

The next day I walked through those doors nervous and afraid. Someone asked, "Can I help you?"

I almost choked, but I said, "Yes."

My interview came, and we chatted for a few moments and then he said, "Once you are done filling out the application, send for me."

Here I was sitting in this room by myself but not seeing the blessing in my present situation.

I forgot all about *the box*.

I began filling out the application. My mind was on making sure I accurately and professionally answered everything correctly.

Another God moment.

There were only four pages of the application, so I finished rather quickly. Once I was done fear hit me like a mac truck going full speed. That voice said, "Kevin, did you check *the box*?" I couldn't remember, and I was afraid to look. But I had to. I nervously glanced at the first page, then the second page. No box. I checked the third page. So many thoughts were running through my mind. I searched the fourth page too.

Nothing was there.

I started my search all over again ending with the same results; 'the box' wasn't on any of the pages!

I thought something must be wrong. I was at a loss for words. I didn't know what to think.

Finally, I had to accept the fact that 'the box' wasn't on the application. I couldn't even thank God for *a God moment* because I didn't understand what it meant.

I got up, turned the application in, and was told to report to work the next month.

Just like that, look at God.

It really didn't hit me until later after talking with my mom and sister. They were excited about it.

Quickly I realized, I had a small problem. Now that I was about to start working for the governor, what would I wear? I didn't have the proper attire that people wore in an office environment. I called my mother and sister, and we met up at Saver's (A donation store). I could not afford all new suits, ties and shoes. That stuff costs a lot. I'm glad my family knew about discount stores like Savers.

The lesson I learned is this, "Always be ready so you don't have to get ready."

I couldn't believe it. I was working for the governor of the state. I was in disbelief. Things were happening fast. I think I'm the first in my family or community to work for a governor in Arkansas. Don't quote me on that though.

The first day of work came so fast. I remember walking through those doors of the Arkansas State Capitol heading to my suite thinking, "Is this really happening?"

Always remember the devil comes to kill, steal, and destroy. It didn't take long for him to make his first move.

As I sat at my desk excited about being there, the devil reminded me that I had a felony and when the background check came back they were going to let me go.

The bottom fell out and was replaced with fear on top of fear. From that day on, I came to work worried about receiving my walking papers. Every day was part happy, part sad because I knew it was going to happen.

I forgot all about the fact that God opens doors no man can close. I was too busy thinking about the bad. I worried too much, and I couldn't share my fear with no one. I lived in fear for a long time early on, and it was tough. It affected my work. I forgot all about that (Isaiah 41:10).

Weeks and then months passed and one day I thought, "Maybe they didn't run a background check on me."

A weight was lifted off my chest and I worried no more.

Thank God!

I began to breath normal again and started feeling better about my blessing. That joy lasted a short time because days later, another joy stealing question surfaced. "What are you going to do when someone you know tell others about you working for the governor?"

It wasn't that I thought people were hating on me. I knew they were just proud that they knew someone who overcame the challenges I had overcome.

My mother told all her friends and church members and anyone that would listen. She was proud of what God had done for me.

How could I tell her to stop telling people about her son's blessing?

What was I going to do if I was out in the community with the Governor and saw someone I knew?

I started thinking about all those scenarios in my head. The devil was dropping seed after seed trying to stop what God had planned for me.

Why wasn't I quoting Romans 8: 28: *And we know that all things work together for good to them that love God, to them who are the called according to his purpose.*

Whenever I was out and saw someone I knew I would quickly caution him or her, "Hey, these people don't know anything about me."

The reason I would do that is because if you knew my friends and family, they were going to be loud and proud to see me.

I did that so many times for the next few years. I was living in fear. Fear became the routine, and I became less comfortable telling people. Again, I was always worried about what if someone shared my story with a coworker.

Some people couldn't help but to celebrate my blessing even if I was afraid to. I'm glad they did.

"Thank yall!"

I gave hope to a lot of people by them seeing how far I came. It was something special about my walk. I remember being somewhere and the Holy Spirit reminded me that God opened that door for me, and when He was ready to close the door, He would. The Holy Spirit tells you of everything God has said (John 14:26).

That was the best news I had heard since joining the governor's office. I had too little faith. I was consumed by what the devil shared with me. Fear blinded me. I couldn't relish the blessing that I was living!

God said, "He will never leave you nor forsake you." (Hebrew 13:5)

From that day forward, I walked in faith every moment. Praise God. Instead of being afraid, I started sharing my God story more and more with people. I kind of felt like it was what God wanted me to do. I took baby steps.

In the governor's office, God put me in a room surrounded by people that I would never have been able to have a relationship with on my own. He showed favor over my life.

I started off as a Communication Assistant making coffee, running errands, directing phone calls, and filing papers for more than two years. I never complained.

One day I was summoned to the deputy director's office for some apparent reason.

Yes, I was nervous, but I contained my fears. I walked through the door of my Deputy of Chief Staff, and the Director of Communication was in there. I didn't know what to think, but I knew that God was in control.

They told me I was doing a good job and that my talent was necessary in representing the governor in the community. In my mind, I wondered, "Did they just promote me?"

I hugged both of them and began praising God. During my time there I received two promotions. How could I doubt, ever?

My opportunity to know God grew. He taught me so much more about Himself. He showed me how to be faithful. He put me around Christians. I was reading the word more. I started praying more. I started acknowledging God. I started being faithful and obedient, not perfect, but I just started to do more of the things that God wanted me to do.

I was growing. I was maturing, and my faith level increased. He took my faith from just an *ordinary* person who believed to an *above average* person who now believed in God's supernatural powers.

I started speaking it!

I still wasn't 100% obedient, but I was obedient. I listened. I recognized the Holy Spirit. I recognized I couldn't have gotten where I was without God.

God just started showing up more and more. He was directing me to here and there. There was so much that God was doing for me during that time. He kept leading me, and I kept noticing that it was God. I praised Him and thanked Him. I started paying my tithes more, giving offerings and sacrificing my mind and body. My maturity level went up, and it was all God. It was just God within me. The God in me cultivated the person that I am today.

This had nothing to do with Kevin, my friends or anyone. This was all God changing my way of thinking and my way of believing. He kept people around me who always said, "God. God. God."

My mother was on me. My grandmother had already passed, but I remembered those 'God moments' that she left with me. My great-grandmother had already passed, but I remember her reading and having that Bible with her at all times. I know they will be in Heaven with me!

God continued to love on me.

During my time in the governor's office, God allowed some things to happen in my life that kept me humble and drew me closer to Him. The closer I got to Him, the more I learned about Him and myself.

So when I faced what I felt to me like another impossible task, God reminded me of what He'd done for me the last time and that he's going to see me through.

Trust me there were some tough times, but God just kept reassuring me, "Hey Kevin, I got you here. Can't nobody open a door that I close, and can't nobody close a door that I open."

He had to keep telling me that, and He kept putting people around me when times got tough in the governor's office. He kept Christian people around me like Patricia Drone-Oliver (thank you for letting God use you when I needed you at work), Mrs. Annie Abrams, my Spiritual-Mother, my good friends Sanci Richardson, Frank Batemen, and Howard Himmbulam, and so many more. God was using them to keep encouraging 'poor little me.'

God knew exactly what I needed and at the right time. He put my now wife Maggie F. Hunt in my path. She has made being married to her everything I dreamed it to be. She supported me when I only had an idea, and she continues to encourage all of my God-visions.

Mrs. Hunt, you are a blessing God placed in my life to grow in Christ with. I'm so glad that you said, "Yes." Thank you for not judging me and for loving me more than I ever imagined. #mydreamwife

Today, my relationship with God is so amazing. I love Him. I trust Him. I know His word is true. I know He is a healer. I know He is a God that knows everything and sees everything. He is omniscient. He is a great God. I'm so thankful He is a part of my life and I know I'm going to Heaven.

I know Christ is interceding for me sitting at the right hand of the throne of God Almighty (Romans 8:34). I'm thankful. I'm grateful. I know He exists. I know Christ lived and died and rose on the third day with all power in His hands.

Why Me God?

I know God told us to go out and make disciples (Matthew 28:19). The God, who sees and knows everything, has continued to see me through all things I've been through. I know that everything I'm doing now is what He put inside me. I know exactly what I'm doing. God has revealed it to me. God has shown it to me. I see myself in many places speaking. I see my book being read. I see myself talking and being a mentor to young men and women and even older men and women; telling them my God story and how God covered me, loved on me even while I was questioning why He chose me.

God revealed to me that this is what He wanted me to do. He told me that this is how He wanted me to do it. Every time I went somewhere to speak I was nervous and I said to God, "God this is not me." Even though I may have felt like I stumbled, I realized it was just preparing me for the next one. The next time I went, it prepared me for the next one.

I didn't realize that I had spoken so many places until one day I looked up and took notice. I realized it couldn't have been nobody but God because there is no way that a person like me (who didn't have the qualifications to be a speaker, or the skill set or techniques to present a powerful speech) could have done this.

God just said, "Tell them your story. Tell them who you are and what I've done for you. Let that be the testimony. Let that be the power. Let that be the powerful testimony of your life."

So, I know that I could not have been working in the governor's office for eight years without anyone knowing that I had been in prison. The only people who knew were the people I told. I know that was only God who kept and covered me.

Kevin L. Hunt, Sr.

One thing I know is that God will use the things we consider hopeless and impossible and turn them into an *only God could have did that* experience.

The things I endured and the blessings I received were not for me; they were for the people that may have traveled the road I have or struggled during the process of a blessing.

This is my God story; and it's about how God had a plan for my life even when I didn't have one myself. But it wasn't for my benefit. It was so I could tell people that He is in the business of directing your path. All you have to do is trust Him during the process.

Only God gets the glory.

God has shown me what He wants me to say and how He wants me to do it. He is showing me what I'm going to do with this book. He has shown me who is going to need this book. He has shown me who will be encouraged and who will be loved by this book.

My relationship with God is amazing!

It is really a God and son relationship. It is based on the foundation of my Lord and Savior Jesus Christ. I know it has to be God who has set me up to be in this position. The beginning has just begun. I know it has to be God because it wasn't me.

I'm so thankful for what He has done and what He is doing. I'm grateful for how powerful He is.

I pray. I trust. I speak. I know God is in control. He tells me. He shows me. He has given me a revelation. He has given me wisdom, knowledge, and understanding. He allows me to discern things. I know it's God and I trust Him.

Why Me God?

Here's another God moment:

When I was still in the governor's office, I went to speak at First Baptist Church in North Little Rock, where Reverend Williams Robinson is the pastor, for a friend name Ms. Louise Scott. I spoke to a youth group and shared my story. They gave me a book entitled *Grace,* written by Max Lucado.

The book was all about the concept of grace. That book led me to the peace of God. As I read about the grace of God, I was inspired to learn more about the peace of God. I realized I hadn't really understood the peace of God. That knowledge prepared me for what was coming.

God knows everything and He will prepare you for what He knows.

God knew that I was going to go to the governor to ask for a pardon. He knew the governor would say yes, but He also knew that I wasn't going to be able to be pardoned. So when I found out I wasn't going to get the pardon, God had already prepared me so that when I heard that bad news, I didn't give up on God. I didn't break down by the news. I didn't lose hope.

What God did was teach me to live in the peace of God.

So when I got to that point of disappointment, it was a blessing because although it bothered me, it didn't bother me like I knew it could have if I had not tapped into God's peace.

When I tapped into that peace, I remember hearing God as clear as if it was just yesterday. He told me, "You don't need a pardon to be successful. You are already successful." I went in after that.

Why Me God?

I had to look back at my life. God reminded me that I was successful. God reminded me of what He had brought me through. He reminded me of where He had taken me, and He reminded me of where I was going.

Because I was prepared with His peace, I could stay empowered and connected to God, even through some tough, bad news.

I was able to continue to love on God and God continued to love on me.

It was amazing, and I was blessed!

Conclusion

Why Me God?

It Isn't About Me

I just shared with you how God's grace opened doors for me, and how He didn't allow my fears, past, or lack of faith, keep Him from blessing my walk.

There were many times I wanted to give up just to go back to what I was familiar with, but God would not allow me to. He kept encouraging me internally and externally.

His grace opened so many doors that no man would have willfully allowed me to enter.

What governor in the world would have allowed someone with a felony to work in his office? Not one.

Why Me God?

God loves a willful spirit.

Once I invested my mind and started to trust in God and meditated on His word, things really became clearer about His perfect will for me (Jeremiah 28:11, Roman 8:28).

I often wonder, "Why would God chose a person like me for such an assignment?"

I had very limited communication, reading, and writing skills. Street terminology was the best I could offer and my confidence in those spaces was hopeless. I never thought that I would be able to do any of the things I've done. But God had a plan for me, for my life in His will.

Why did he choose me?

Only God could have open doors that set me on track to obtain a GED, bachelor and master degrees, and work in the governor's office. Only

God could have orchestrated for me to be the keynote speaker at GED graduations throughout Arkansas, church youth programs, stop the violence conferences and mentor to area boys and girls clubs. Only God opened those doors. I embrace Romans 12:2.

I'm not trying to tell you how to live, but I am trying to tell you who you can trust and remind you that God opens the door no man can close, and He closes doors no man can open.

Once God revealed my calling to me, I questioned it.

I knew that there were others more qualified than I was. I had friends that went through some of the same things I've been through, but were better speakers, writers, spellers and even had the confidence to go out to do the work and some have. So, I asked, "Why me God?"

I hated my calling for a long time. Thinking about it frustrated me. I wanted to do other things with my life. It didn't make sense to me. I didn't want to tell people my story, so I started coming up with any reason why I couldn't speak. I stopped answering emails and phone calls. I was running.

I used to hate when people would ask me to come share a few words or be their keynote speaker. I fought my calling for a long time, until one day God opened up my eyes to see the good I would be doing.

I finally understood that my walk is not just for me; it's for people that have faced some of the similar challenges I have.

There are many people who can benefit from hearing my God success story. How selfish of me for not willingly giving God the glory He deserves by telling people what He did for me.

Kevin L. Hunt, Sr.

Why Me God?

My mind and body decided I would always tell my story. I would freely tell people how His grace covered me and that He alone deserves the glory.

If there are tangible or intangible obstacles that have made you doubt that you can or if you really want to change your life, you can use my story as proof that it can be done.

If you know someone that may have had a string of tough luck in their lives, tell them it's not over because we serve a God that changed water into wine.

And if that is still hard to conceive, I want you to tell them about a person that could not read, spell, write, or speak. He came from a low-income family, was a gang banger, spent time in jail, didn't know God, and only had a street education. He dropped out of middle school. I want you to tell them about Kevin L. Hunt Sr. I want you to pass this book on to them.

Tell them, it's never too late to rewrite their story.

God always listens and responds in His perfect timing.

I know why God choose me… "Because He Ordained My Steps."

Follow me

Twitter, Instagram, Facebook:

@klhuntsr

Photos

Figure 1 (left to right) Mrs. Maggie F. Hunt, Mrs. Bennie (Yeargin) Waller, Mrs. Pauline Bowles, Author Kevin L. Hunt, Sr.

Figure 2 Kevin L. Hunt, Jr.

Figure 3 Mentor: (left to right) Mr. Howard Himmelbaum and Author Kevin L. Hunt, Sr.

Figure 4 (left to right) Author Kevin L. Hunt, Sr., Mrs. Annie Abrams, Mrs. Sanci Richardson

Figure 5 Ms. Pamela Boykins and Author Kevin L. Hunt, Sr.

About the Author

Kevin L. Hunt Sr. dropped out of school in junior high. His life went into a downward spiral for many years afterward. Unable to support himself due to his lack of education, Kevin relied on his family for their financial support.

In 2001, he made a decision that would be the catalyst for changing his entire life; he enrolled in Shorter College GED program.

After earning his GED in 2001, Kevin courageously enrolled in Philander Smith College in 2002, where he not only received a Business Degree in 2005 but graduated with honors. He went on to receive a master's degree in December of 2015 from Webster's University.

Upon graduating from Philander Smith College, Kevin volunteered for then Arkansas Attorney General Mike Beebe's campaign for governor. This eventually led to a part-time job working for Beebe's campaign. Mike Beebe won the election for Governor (2006), and Kevin was hired on as full-time staff.

During the next eight years in the office of Governor Mike Beebe, Kevin worked as communication assistant, spending five of those years as Minority Affairs Liaison.

Kevin invests countless hours of hard work and dedication for the betterment of his community by serving as a mentor to others and volunteering for friend and mentor, Reverend Hezekiah Stewart and the Watershed.

Currently, he is focused on launching his nonprofit mentoring program, Inspiring Other

People (IOP), whose motto is "Leading By Example."

A man of God, Kevin joined Second Baptist Church in 2005, under the leadership of Pastor, Dr. Kevin A. Kelly.

Kevin Hunt Sr., a native of Little Rock Arkansas. He is the son of a very strong mother, father, grandmother and great-grandmother. He is also the proud father of one son, Kevin Hunt Jr. He is married to Maggie F. Hunt - the love of his life, a blessing from God himself.

EIFFEL TOWER BOOKS

An Imprint of

Butterfly Typeface Publishing

Butterfly Typeface Publishing is a professional editing, writing and publishing company. Our goal is to 'spread a message' of inspiration, imagination and intrigue in all that we do. Whether you hire us to edit, ghostwrite, publish (books & magazines) or web design, you can be guaranteed exemplary customer service, fairness and quality. Our vision, under God's leadership, is to serve and assist in the healing of the heart, mind and soul of *all* people we encounter with integrity, intentional influence and positive purpose.

"We make good GREAT!"
Iris M Williams – Owner
PO Box 56193
Little Rock Arkansas
72215